THE ART OF GRAINING

THE ART OF GRAINING

CHARLES PICKERT,
A. METCALF

ISBN: 978-93-90015-08-5

Published: 1872

LECTOR HOUSE LLP
E-MAIL: lectorpublishing@gmail.com

THE ART OF GRAINING:

HOW ACQUIRED AND HOW PRODUCED. WITH DESCRIPTION OF COLORS AND THEIR APPLICATIONS. WITH LITHOGRAPHIC ILLUSTRATIONS OF THE VARIOUS WOODS USED IN INTERIOR FINISHING.

BY

CHARLES PICKERT AND A. METCALF.

WITH 42 COLORED PLATES ON STONE.

1872.

CONTENTS

INTRODUCTION.

The Art of Graining is judged by the authors of this treatise to be of sufficient importance to justify a work devoted especially to the task of giving instruction to learners of the art.

All graining is an imitation of some more or less well known wood, and the learner may doubtless draw from nature the copies he desires to imitate; but it is only trained skill that can accomplish the task perfectly, and it is presumably true that those who, in acquiring a long experience, have made the obstacles to success a special study, are best prepared to afford instruction to a beginner.

The authors of the work present here the result of a long experience in the practice of this decorative art, and feel confident that they hereby offer to their brother artisans a reliable guide to improvement in the practice of graining.

It is earnestly recommended by the authors that learners should practise drawing the several copies given as samples, with drawing pencils, using both narrow and broad-pointed, as the surest means of acquiring such thorough mastery of proper manipulation as will insure the highest degree of success.

It is believed, moreover, that experienced learners will find it not amiss to avail themselves of the methods set forth in this treatise, affording as they do, the sum of the examples of fellow-artisans who have carefully studied nature's own modes, and have studiously followed such plans in working as insured the closest and most durable adherence to the original form and color.

CHARLES PICKERT,
A. METCALF.

INSTRUCTIONS

HOW TO MIX AND APPLY THE COLORS IN GRAINING THE VARIOUS WOODS HEREIN REPRESENTED.

As oak and black walnut are the principal woods imitated in graining, we have given them a prominent place and careful attention in our work, for when the ability to produce imitations of *those* properly is once thoroughly attained, the graining of other woods becomes a comparatively easy task.

First:—In preparing work for graining, great attention should be given to the shellacking of all knots and other parts containing any inequalities of surface, whether from the exudation of pitch, gum, or other substance; unless this precaution is observed the pitch or gum will force itself through a great many coats of paint.

OAK.

Illustrations of OAK include Plates 1-17.

For oak-graining the priming coat should be white, mixed (not too thickly) with pure lead and linseed-oil; then, when thoroughly dry, and ready for a second coat of paint, much care should be observed in well stopping or puttying with white lead or common putty, as may be thought best, leaving all nail-holes or other inequalities well filled, pressed in and rounded up, so that when thoroughly sand-papered it will leave the surface entirely smooth and level. For a second coat of paint, a little yellow chrome or Rochelle may be added, sufficient to make it a light cream color, using for a body pure lead, turpentine, oil, and a small quantity of japan, making the paint a trifle thicker than the priming coat, having it well mixed and strained, so that it shall not contain any lumps or foreign substance. Here let us say that the habit of undertaking to do graining work on two coats of paint is entirely wrong; good work cannot by any possibility be performed unless there shall have been at least three coats laid on as a foundation, — otherwise it will not wipe out clean, but will appear muddy and foul when completed.

For a third coat of grained work, if a very light oak is desired, add to the same mixture of lead, oil, etc., sufficient yellow as before, to produce a delicate cream, adding to that a very small quantity of American vermilion, or Venetian red. After laying on the second coat, the work should be well and carefully sand-papered, puttying (as before suggested), if necessary. When the third coat has been on two or more days, and has become thoroughly hard and dry, use upon the surface very fine sand-paper, so that a perfectly smooth finish may be obtained.

For light-oak graining-color, use equal parts of raw umber and raw Sienna, and if a little darker shade is desired, tone with burnt umber, grinding into the same a little *Paris*, or common *whiting*, which gives it body and holds it together. A little beeswax or brown Windsor soap dissolved in turpentine may be used if desired, but in a small quantity.

For mixing the colors employ one-fourth boiled oil, three-fourths turpentine, adding for drier a very little japan. Graining-colors should invariably stand from six to ten hours after mixing before being applied, and if too thick, when adding the thinners be cautious to avoid stirring from the bottom. The colors should be mixed to such a consistency, that when put on, a perfectly clear and transparent appearance may be obtained. For darker shades of oak, more yellow and red should be used in the ground-work and more burnt umber in the graining-color, adding enough of the burnt umber to make the graining-color harmonize with the ground-work. And here we would suggest that every grainer, who desires to perfect himself in the art, should procure small pieces of the various kinds of wood he wishes to imitate, and in all cases mix his colors in harmony with those shown in the wood—mixing his ground-work so as to compare with the *lightest* shade observable in the wood.

Too much care cannot be taken in the *preparation* of graining-colors; more failures have been made through neglect of this, than in the execution of the work itself, for except the colors are in proper harmony with the wood desired to be imitated, the work, though well executed, must be a failure in the production of the wished-for object.

For the last coat of the ground-work for oak, there should be a sufficiency of oil to impart a slight gloss when laid on, which enables it to be wiped clean, free, and unclouded.

For *shading* oak use a little raw Sienna, raw and burnt umber, mixing with oil, turpentine, japan, etc., as before mentioned. Where knots or curls occur in the grain, as shown in our illustration, there light and careless shades should be thrown in, avoiding anything prominent or harsh, and in most cases make the growth or heart slightly darker than at the edge. A beautiful effect can be produced by combing over the flaking with a fine or coarse rubber comb, blending very lightly in the same direction the veins or comb take. The effect produced is to sink the flaking, making it look solid and true to nature.

For wiping out oak (as in samples shown), see description of process in our following chapter on black walnut, using the same tools, etc. (rubber combs, English or American steel combs in oak, not in walnut). Where flaking is done it is combed first with a coarse, then a fine steel comb, but where heart or growth-pieces occur, no comb should be used until wiped out, then comb with a fine comb very lightly in the same direction the grains may run.

In graining, particularly oak, care should be taken to have the grains lose themselves regularly at the sides, not leaving the heart-piece abruptly, but gradually (as shown in our illustration), preserving a proper harmony of colors from centre to outside.

BLACK WALNUT.

Illustrations of WALNUT include Plates 18-28.

The same care should be taken in puttying, sand-papering, mixing, and applying, as hereinbefore suggested in the chapter upon graining oak.

The ground-work for black walnut should be mixed with pure white lead, turpentine, oil, japan, etc., colored with chrome yellow or good Rochelle ochre, American vermilion, or English Venetian red, and burnt umber, which if properly combined produces the most proper ground-work attainable. This wood varies in color, some pieces bearing upon the yellow, and others upon the red, either of which may be correctly imitated by adding yellow or red as the case requires. There are some pieces, however, of a grayish cast, and if such a characteristic is desired in graining, add to the ground-work a little Vandyke brown.

The ground-work (last coat) should be so mixed as to have, when dry, an egg-shell gloss, in order to prevent the first coat of graining (which is "distemper-color") from crawling or running together. Black walnut is a very porous wood, and unless the pores are properly shown in the graining, the imitation will be far from perfect; no grainer, therefore, should depart so far from nature as to omit this necessary and absolute consideration.

For the accomplishment of a correct imitation in this respect, take a small quantity of sour or common ale, or, if not obtainable, a little vinegar and water (equal parts) will do (urine is an excellent substitute for either of the liquids named), and to this add, for coloring purposes, three-fourths burnt umber and one-fourth Vandyke brown; when this is applied, and before dry, take a dry brush (a flat one is preferable), and "whip" the color thoroughly with the same, keeping the hand close to the surface of the object to be grained; and as pores in some pieces of walnut show far more distinctly than in others, to imitate this, certain portions should be whipped very coarsely, while other portions should be whipped very fine. Care must be taken in whipping, to have all joints, etc., left perfectly square as constructed, and the whipping should invariably be done as the grain of the wood is designed to run. The distemper-color should be mixed to a thickness, that, when applied and properly whipped, the general tone of the ground-work shall not be materially changed.

Some grainers, before proceeding further in graining black walnut, have varnished the distemper-coat; we regard this as entirely useless, as well as detrimental to the general tone of the graining when done. The impression current among some painters, that when the graining-color is applied to the distemper-color, without first varnishing, it (the distemper-color) will rub up, is erroneous, for when perfectly dry it is all ready to receive the graining-color.

After complying with the foregoing directions, the article being now all ready for graining, having, as shown, received the distemper-color, take three-fourths burnt umber and one-fourth Vandyke brown, mixed with three-fourths turpentine, one-fourth oil and japan, using beeswax or soap to prevent its running as in oak-graining (of course the color must be varied to comply with the ground-work by adding burnt umber, Vandyke brown, or burnt Sienna, as hereinbefore set forth in our directions for oak-graining), and to avoid darkening the graining but a very little, the color should be used thin.

In graining a panel, for instance, in order to obtain a correct imitation of black walnut, the grainer, when running the heart-piece (as shown in our illustrations), should have upon his pallet, glass, or board, a small quantity of umber and Vandyke brown to darken the centre a little, thereby showing the grains perfectly clear in the centre while they lose themselves near the outer edge.

In graining black walnut, combs should be used as little as possible, leaving all the plain parts to be finished in the glazing. For wiping out growths, some use chamois, others use cotton cloths drawn closely over the thumb nail, while many use in place of either, a small piece of rubber, or belting cut about one-fourth of an inch wide at the end used, and in some instances, where a cheap job of graining is desired, rubber combs cut fine and coarse can be used with good success in running growths or hearts by blending lightly after combing.

This brings the work up to a finishing, or shading point, for which purpose use principally Vandyke brown, burnt umber and ivory-black, mixed with oil, turpentine, etc. (as hereinbefore named), and by keeping upon the board, glass or pallet, a little of these separately, and using more of one than the other, a beautiful and correct variety can be produced, it being almost impossible to find two pieces of walnut exactly alike in shade. Like the rest, shading must be applied with a brush, and where crooks, curls, or knots in the grain may appear (see illustrations), careless and light shades should be thrown in, and in the greater number of cases cause growths a trifle darker than edges. For shading the plain parts, a fine and very proper effect will be produced by first applying the color and then by laying on a flat brush, pressing it heavily, and drawing it crooked or straight as desired, then by blending the same very lightly. Where the brush is not thus used, a similar effect can be produced by wiping out lines at small intervals, then blending, in all cases avoiding the too common error of putting *too much work in the graining*, and preserve a proper harmony of colors so that when completed the work will appear rich, clean, and finished.

All graining can be finished by varnishing, or to imitate in "oil-finish" if preferable. Should the latter be desirable take one (1) quart of turpentine; one-fourth (1/4) lb. of white wax (melted in turpentine), adding one half (1/2) pint of best coach varnish (hard drying); one half (1/2) pint of boiled oil, and one (1) gill of japan—apply with a brush, and use sparingly, one coat is sufficient.

By conforming to our directions, in the graining of black walnut, great and satisfactory results will follow.

ROSEWOOD.

Illustrations of ROSEWOOD include Plates 29-31.

In preparing work for rosewood the same instructions should be followed as are laid down in the preceding remarks upon the graining, etc., of black walnut, for the ground-work of both woods is formed of the same colors, only more of the red and yellow is used for rosewood than walnut, as the former varies more in tone between red and yellow. The same rules in both cases should be conformed with, and similar tools in applying or laying on are used. In preparing ground-work for rosewood, however, a little rose pink may sometimes be employed advantageously. Of course the egg-shell gloss must be attained after the third ground-work is laid on, in order to receive the whipping-coat properly.

Pores in rosewood being very fine, the whipping should be as fine as possible. The distemper color is made from burnt umber, a very little Vandyke brown, and a small quantity of rose-pink, ground in ale, or vinegar and water, etc., as before mentioned, and applied very thin. The first coat of graining is mixed from Vandyke brown, burnt umber, and ivory-black (though mainly from the former), ground very fine in oil, turpentine, wax, etc., and must stand after being mixed for some six hours before applying. In some cases, where a reddish cast is desired, it will be well to use a trifle more of the rose-pink.

As the grains in rosewood run very irregularly (see illustration), great care must be maintained in combing, it being necessary in most cases to employ extremely coarse and fine combs; and at times it may be absolutely necessary to use a pencil, in bringing up this imitation to perfection, and all of the combing and pencilling must be blended down very softly with a fine badger blender. For the glazing, the same colors may be used, though chiefly Vandyke brown and ivory-black, making the dark places principally from the latter, though, of course, all of these colors are to be made exceedingly thin and as transparent as possible.

Where a particularly rich finish is desired, a good effect will result by giving the work another extremely thin coat of glazing, composed of rose-pink with a little ivory-black, thus sinking and harmonizing the whole work, giving it a rich and very fine appearance. When the work becomes thoroughly hard and dry, it can be finished either in varnish or oil, as heretofore mentioned in the finishing of black walnut.

MAPLE.

Illustrations of MAPLE include Plates 32-34.

This, though a very beautiful wood, is not as commonly used in graining as some others, though a fine effect can be produced by graining panels, etc., in rooms where the principal graining may be black walnut, oak, or rosewood, forming thus a contrast, which, when well executed, presents an extremely fine appearance, and as maple is never used for an outside finish (therefore not being exposed to the weather), it can be grained more successfully in distemper than in oil, and also much more readily, the consequence of which is, we shall speak of it as being grained only in distemper color, though the same colors, used by a skilful hand, in oil, will produce the same beautiful effect.

The ground-work for maple is made from white, tinted with chrome yellow, making the very lightest cream, and the same rules as to mixing, laying on, etc., etc., are applicable to the graining of maple as to the other woods hereinbefore mentioned, viz., walnut, oak, and rosewood.

The graining color is made from raw Sienna and a little raw umber, not far from equal parts, and ground fine in ale, etc., as before laid down for distemper colors. By rubbing the ground-work upon which all distemper colors are laid, with a damp sponge, it will be found to take the color much more readily than when not so rubbed.

The tools necessary for the graining of maple are a badger-hair blender, two or three top, or over-grainers, varying in width; and in running of heart-pieces, pencils must be used. For making the curls in curly maple, there can be nothing better than a raw potato, cut, say two or three inches wide, with a thin, straight edge, although the work can be performed by using a piece of rubber, or belting, with a similar straight edge. A flat camel's-hair brush, used wet, will accomplish the same, and for this purpose it is employed quite successfully.

In forming the bird's-eyes, a potato cut in two, near the centre, with various inequalities made upon the smooth surface, and carelessly pounced over the surface of the work, will prove successful; but we know of nothing better adapted for this purpose than the ends of the fingers, touching the surface therewith at intervals. (See samples.)

After a thin coating of the distemper is laid on, for the production of curly maple, take a potato, or some one of the other things spoken of, and form the curls by running it crosswise, making them as irregular and careless as possible, then blend them down to a perfect harmony, after which pounce the same with the end of the blender as softly and finely as possible, as the pores in maple are nearly indistinct. After allowing this to dry thoroughly, if a heart or growth is desired, run the same with a pencil as before mentioned, or form the grains by taking the over-grainer, touching it in the color (having combed the grainer before being touched in the color); then run it down over the work, holding the hand near the work; then blend those also carefully, and, especially in maple, avoid anything harsh or stiff in the color, or the running of the grains, as maple, when completed, is a very light and transparent wood. Where bird's-eye-maple is desired (after the thin distemper color has been used), take the damp sponge and roll it carelessly over the surface, which will remove a portion; then blend softly as in forming the curls, after which, and before it is allowed to dry, form the bird's-eye with a potato or fingers, as before mentioned, in those parts where the color has not been removed; then, when entirely dry, form the grains either with a pencil or a grainer, as set forth in directions on curly maple. Care should be taken to have the bird's-eyes shaded (as per illustration), thereby making them natural and complete. After complying with the foregoing instructions, the work is ready for the varnish, and in most cases will be found satisfactorily finished, though it can be materially improved by first giving it a very thin coat of varnish, then a very thin glazing coat of the same colors, though principally of Sienna, forming curls, shades, etc., where they may have been omitted, or will be found to improve the work. You will observe in our illustrations that the grains of maple, both bird's-eye and curly, are entirely different from those of any other kind of wood, both in course and formation. In all cases the illustrations herein given must be followed as closely as possible, which, if properly complied with, will, in all cases, produce the desired result. If desired to be grained in oil, combs should be used instead of top, or over-grainers.

In connection with maple, we would here say that there is such a wood as *satin-wood*, but it is rarely used in any manner.

If, however, it should be desirable to grain it, it will be found that the colors used in graining maple (raw Sienna being the chief material) are the same as those used in the graining of satin-wood, and the process varies in no essential manner, only that the colors and graining should be more indistinct with satin-wood, it being an extremely pale and transparent wood. Care must be observed to preserve in the imitation the purity and character of the original.

ASH.

Illustrations of ASH include Plates 35-38.

A very beautiful and prolific wood, attainable so easily throughout the greater part of the country, is now growing in daily favor for the interior of houses and other buildings, its susceptibility of high finish making it desirable as well as handsome, and probably when well grained it presents more attractiveness than any of the other woods.

Grainers, therefore, should become skilled as far as possible in the imitation of this brilliant and durable wood, and it seems our duty to call especial attention to our illustrations of this wood while endeavoring to impress upon the minds of our readers its adaptability for the purposes herein cited. The ground-work of ash is produced by using a little chrome or Rochelle yellow, together with the least possible tint of red, to which add a trifle of Vandyke brown. But little of this must be used or the ground-work will be too gray. The color when mixed must compare with the lightest shade found in the wood itself. The ground-work must be left with the egg-shell gloss, spoken of in our former chapters. Ash being a very porous wood, the pores, therefore, must, in no case, be left out in the graining, otherwise the work will be incomplete, and for the purpose of producing those take one-half raw umber, one-fourth raw sienna, and one-eighth Vandyke brown; grind all in ale, etc., and apply the same, using it very thin, and whipping it thoroughly, as instructed in directions pertaining to rosewood, etc.

For the second coat, or oil-graining, use the same colors in about the same quantities, ground in oil, turpentine, wax, etc., as mentioned in graining other woods. The same rules as to graining black walnut—darkening the centre a little, and having the grains lose themselves at the sides or ends—are applicable in the graining of ash, and the same tools should also be used in the graining of this wood as are used in that of black walnut; the hand should run the same as in graining walnut, and the grains should run with equal regularity. In *shading*, the same colors may be used, adding a little more Vandyke brown, and grainers, particularly in shading, should study to imitate nature itself in each particular. Of course the colors should be so mixed and strained as to avoid the possibility of their containing harsh or lumpy substances, so that the work will prove to be clean, smooth, and free from any cloudy or impure appearance.

It can be finished in varnish, or in oil, the same as other woods heretofore named.

CHESTNUT.

Illustrations of CHESTNUT include Plates 39-42.

Is largely used, and, like ash, is a particularly beautiful wood. Becoming so well and favorably known for the various purposes to which it can be applied, grainers should study well its beauties, and in their imitation thereof strive to hold the mirror up to nature. The ground-work of chestnut is produced with the same class of colors as that of ash is, only a little more Vandyke brown should be employed, to produce a more grayish tint than is found in ash.

Though chrome is used in the ground-work of chestnut, we deem it inferior to Rochelle yellow, inasmuch as the latter has a more subdued shade, in nearer conformity to chestnut, than that produced by chrome, the latter giving the work a more sprightly hue than is observable in the wood itself. Chestnut is very porous, or rather it shows a more porous condition than ash itself, and to produce this there should be used a little raw umber, raw Sienna, burnt umber, and Vandyke brown, in nearly equal parts, ground in ale, giving the work a very thin coat, and whipping coarsely, so that when done the pores will show very plainly. For the second, or oil-graining, use the same colors, in the same quantities, ground in oil, turpentine, wax, etc., as before instructed. Grain on much the same principle as in ash, only coarser,—the grains in chestnut running much coarser, but yet with the same regularity as those found either in ash or black walnut. For shading chestnut use a little burnt umber and Vandyke brown (rather more of the former), to which add a small quantity of raw Sienna, grinding them in oil, turpentine, etc. In applying this color have it very thin, as in other grainings, and as chestnut is a plain wood, presenting a great uniformity of color in itself, great care must be taken to avoid any material change in the appearance of the graining by any heavy shades.

This rule, it will be observed, is in this regard dissimilar from that laid down to govern the graining of ash, as the latter presents in nature many heavy and eccentric shades, etc., while in the former there is very little diversity in the shade. The same process of wiping out and darkening the centre is applicable to this wood as that set forth to govern in the cases of walnut and ash, similar combs and tools being used in the work upon each and all; and, like the other woods, chestnut can be finished in oil or varnish, as heretofore noted, and when finished is substantial in appearance and very beautiful.

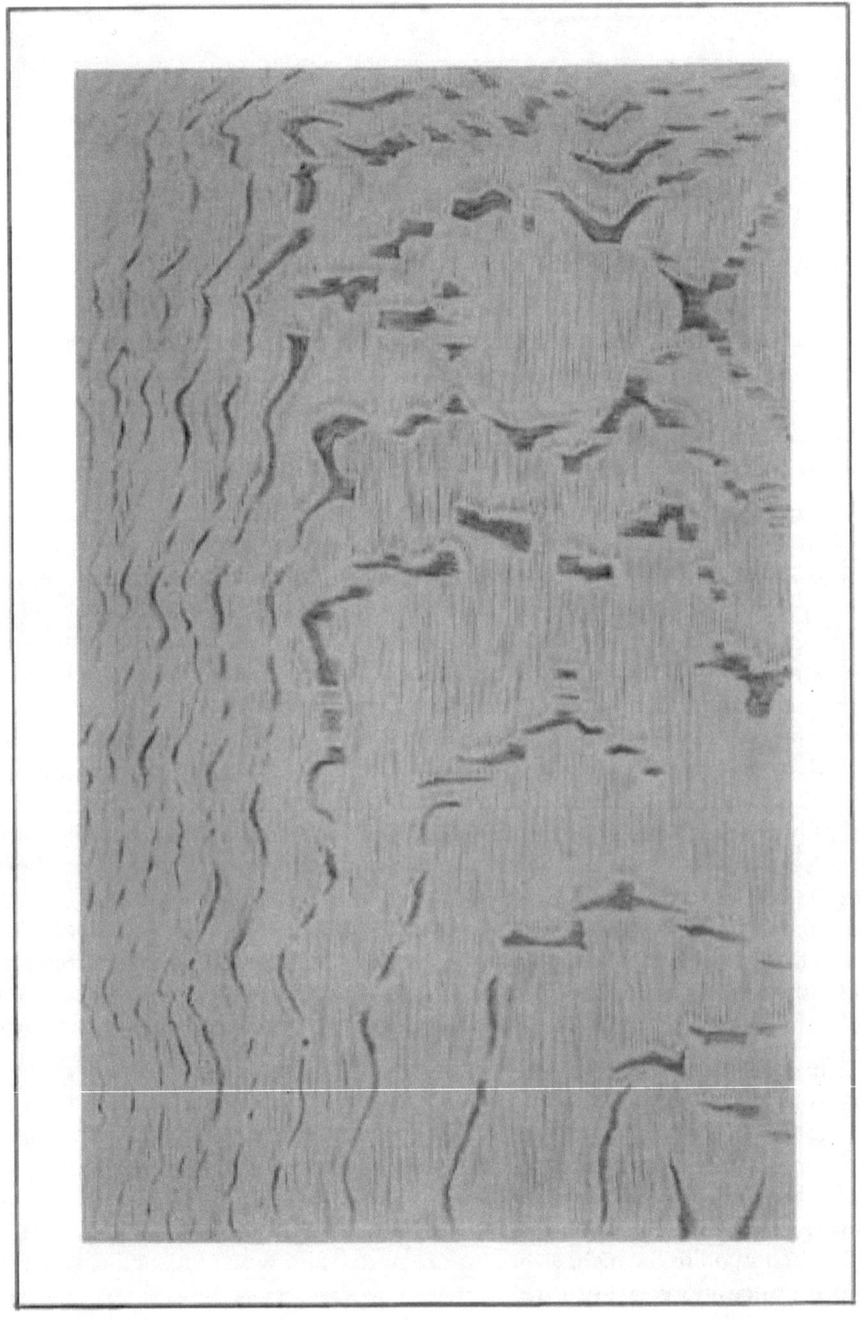

PL. 1

OAK FLAKING.

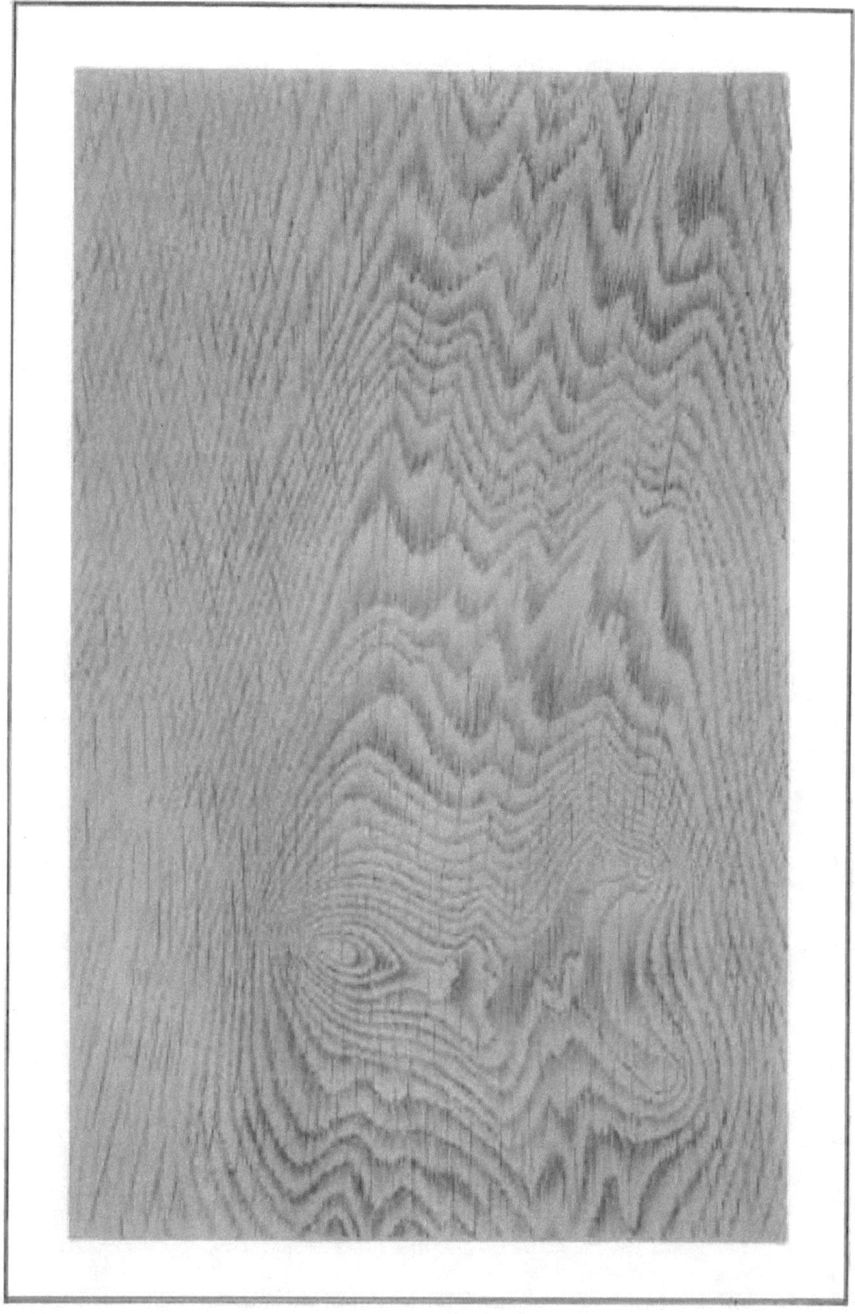

PL. 2

OAK GROWTH.

PL. 3
OAK FLAKING.

PL. 4

OAK GROWTH AND FLAKING.

PL. 5
OAK FLAKING.

PL. 6

OAK GROWTH.

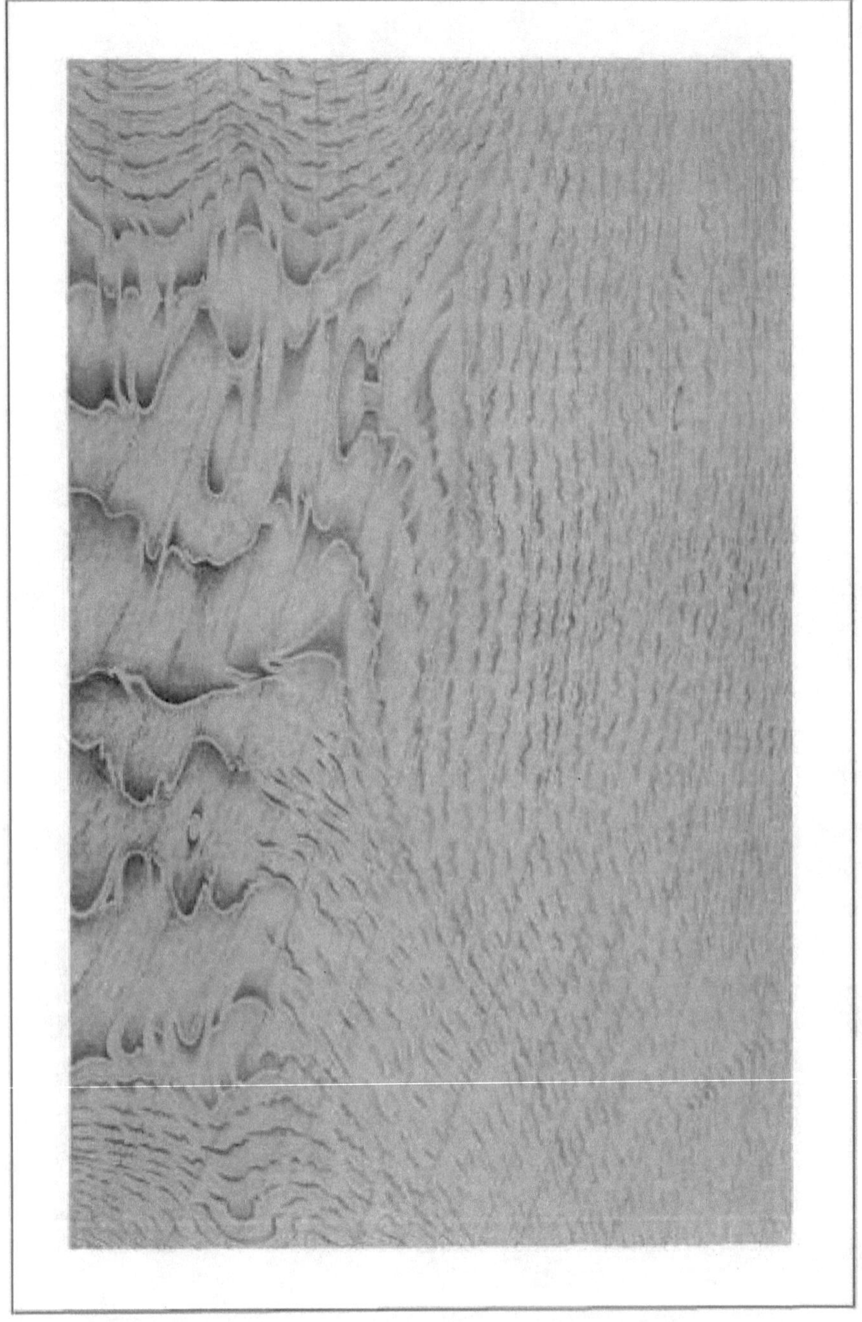

PL. 7

OAK FLAKING.

PL. 8
OAK GROWTH.

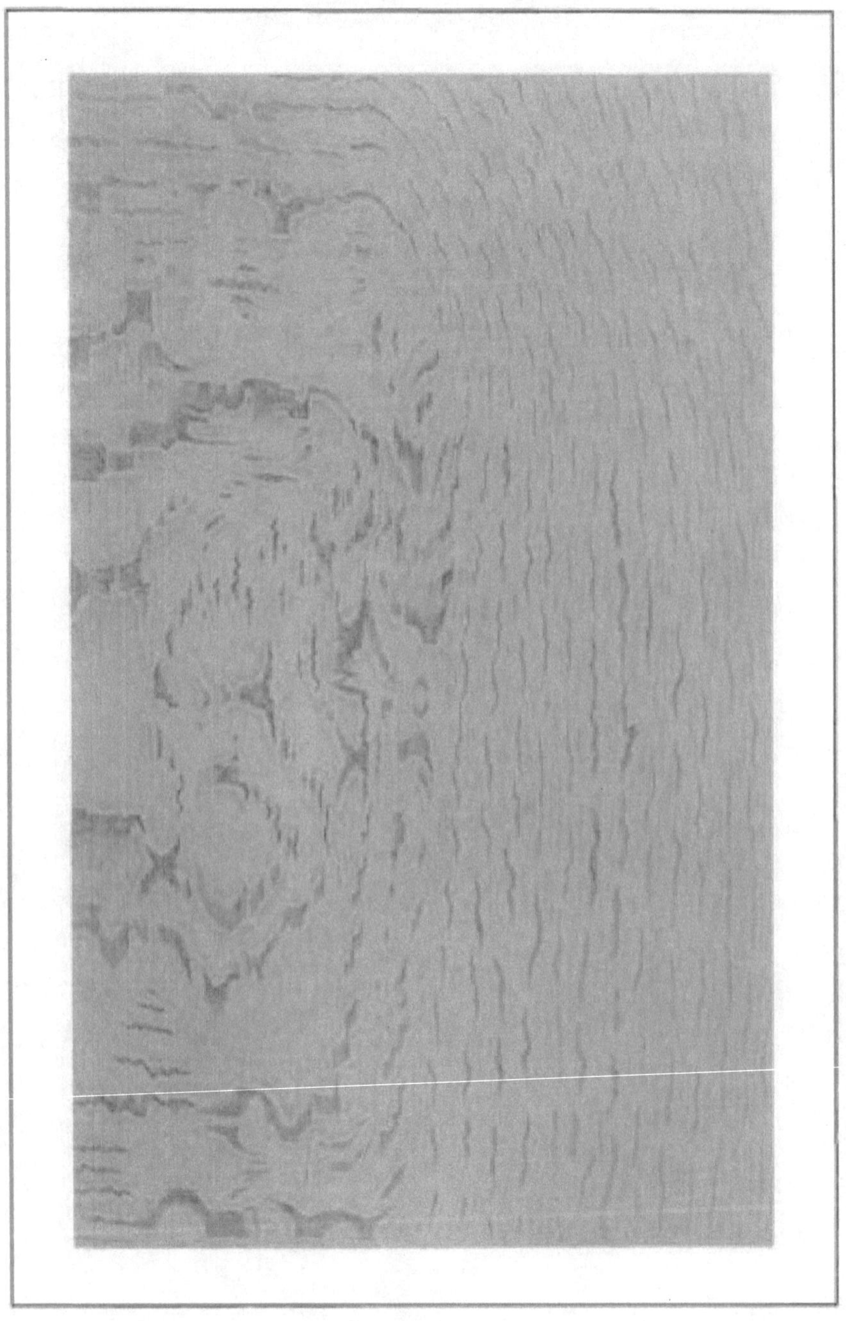

PL. 9

OAK FLAKING.

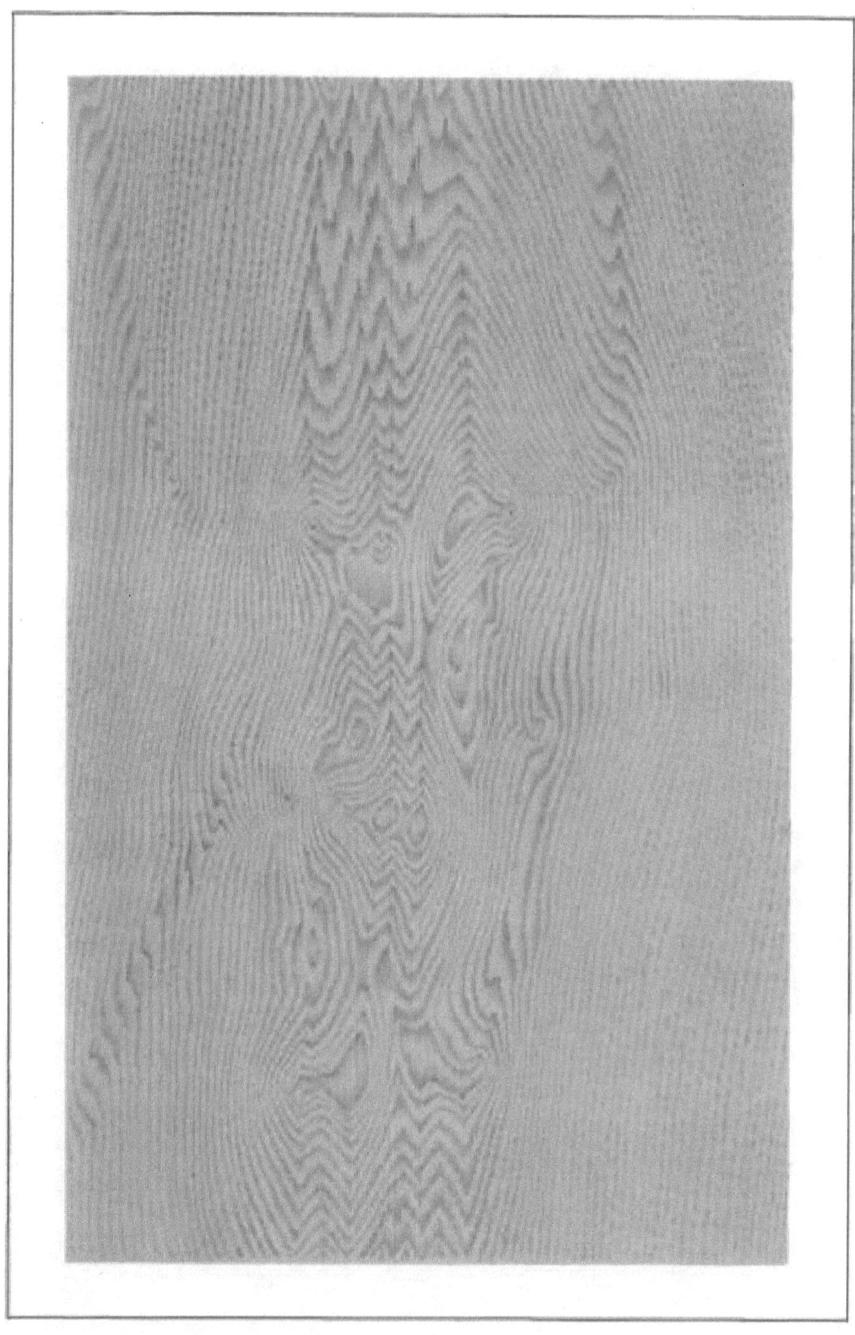

PL. 10

OAK GROWTH.

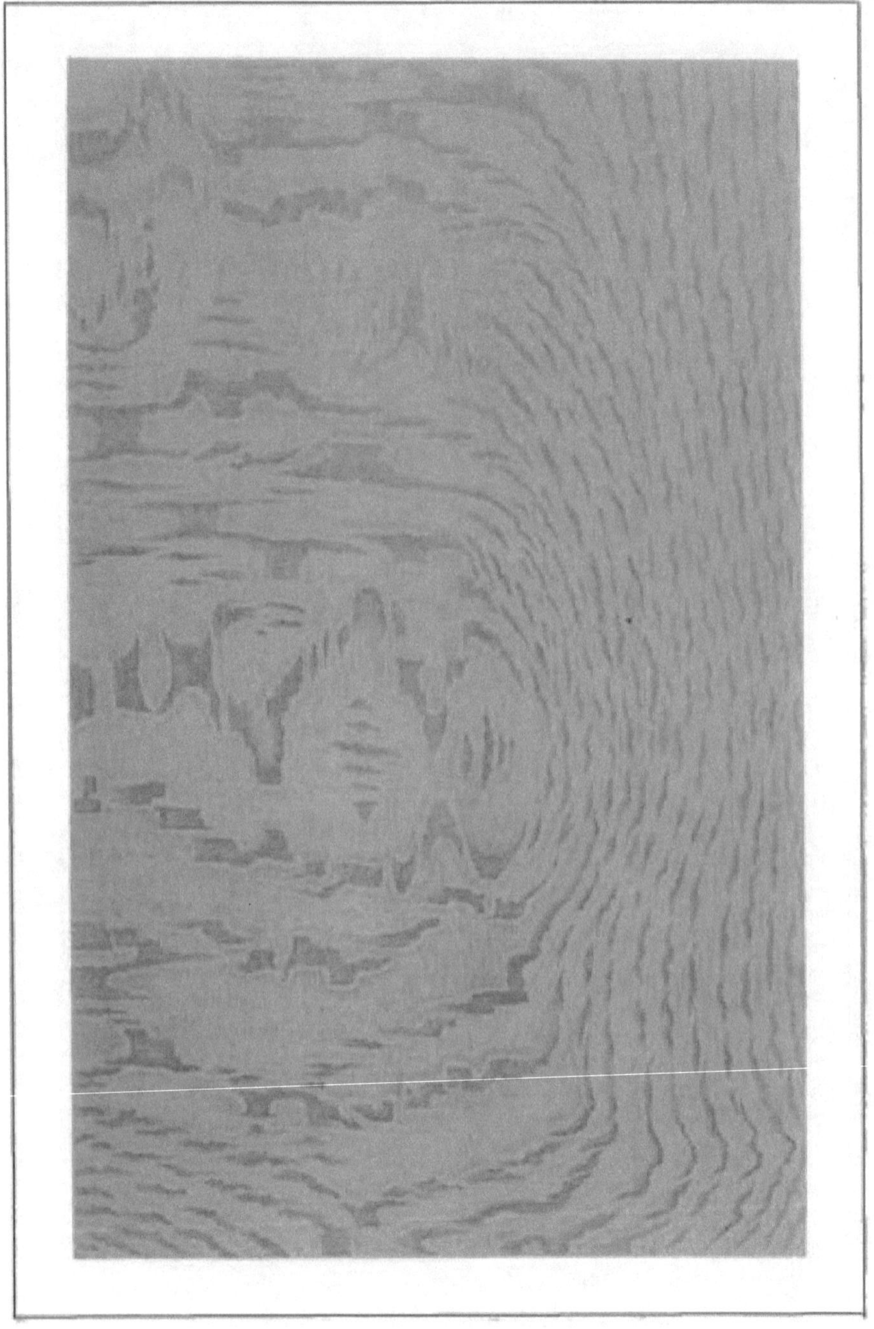

PL. 11

OAK FLAKING.

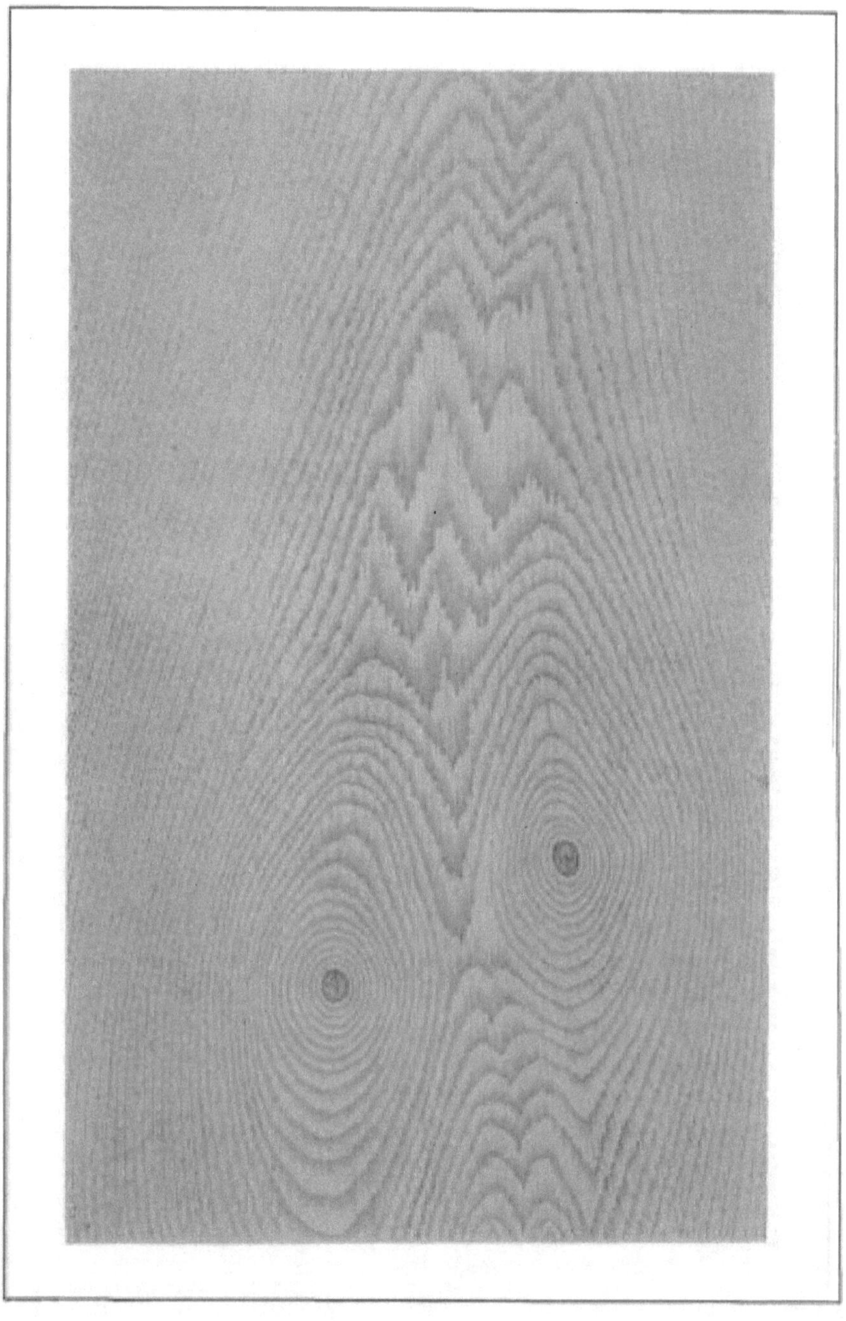

PL. 12

WHITE OAK GROWTH.

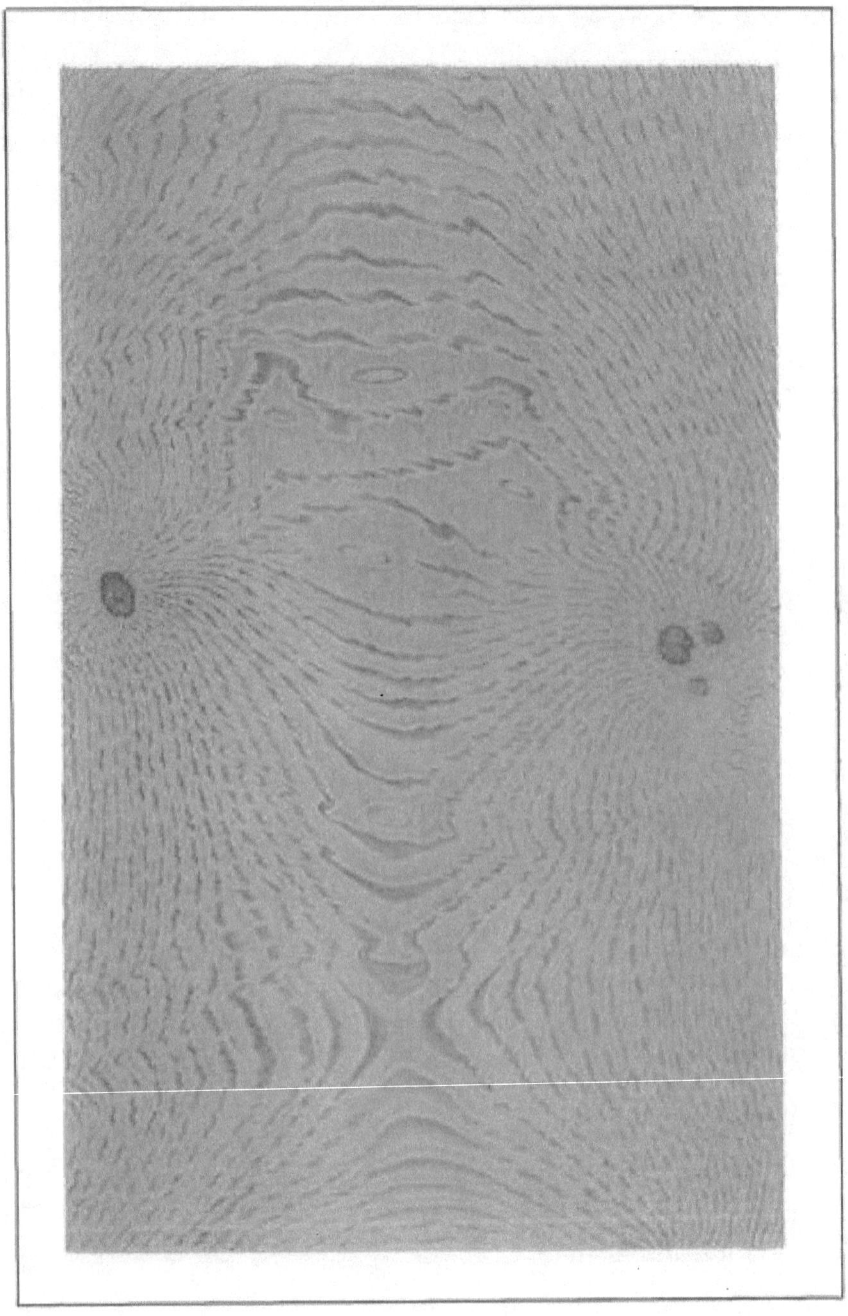

PL. 13

OAK FLAKING.

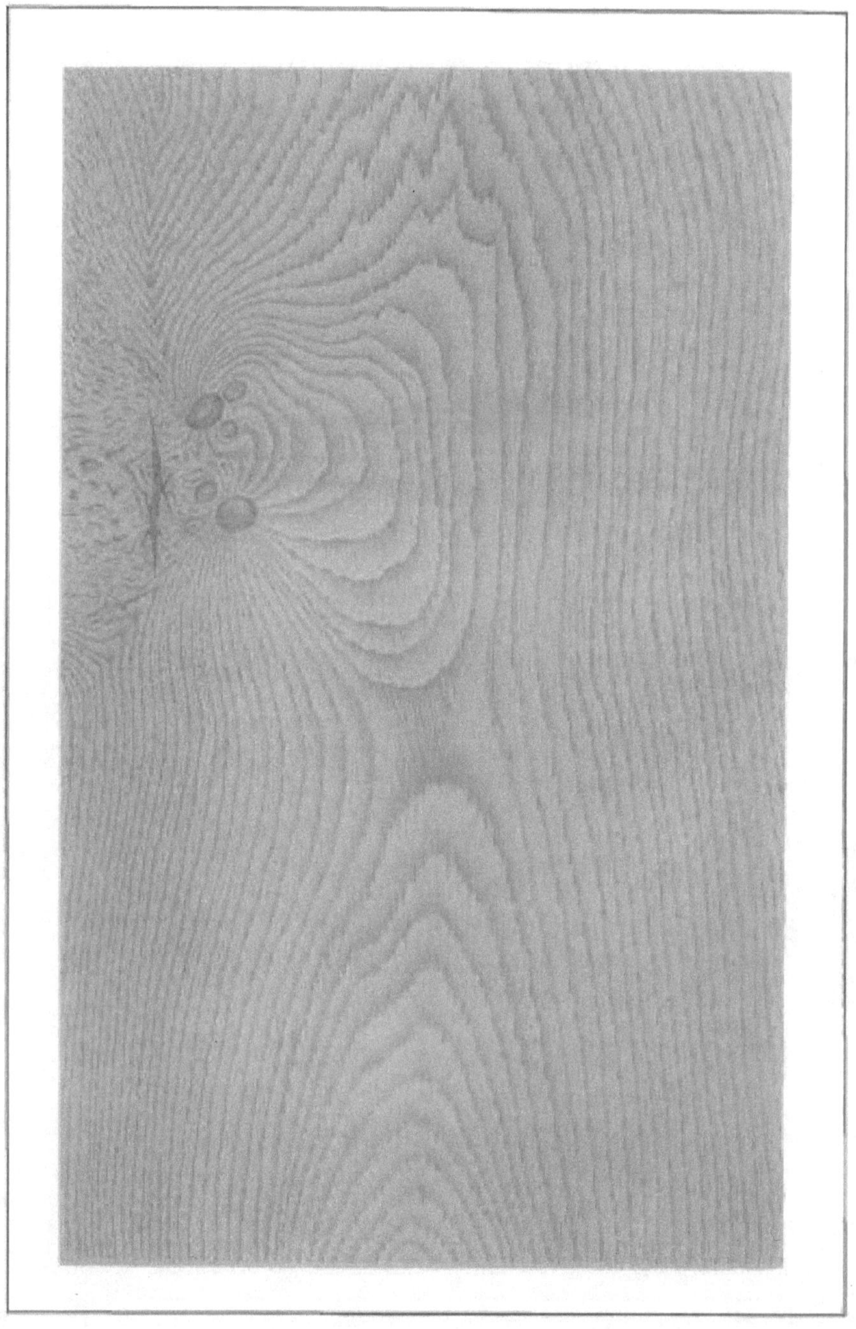

PL. 14

WHITE OAK GROWTH.

PL. 15

OAK FLAKING.

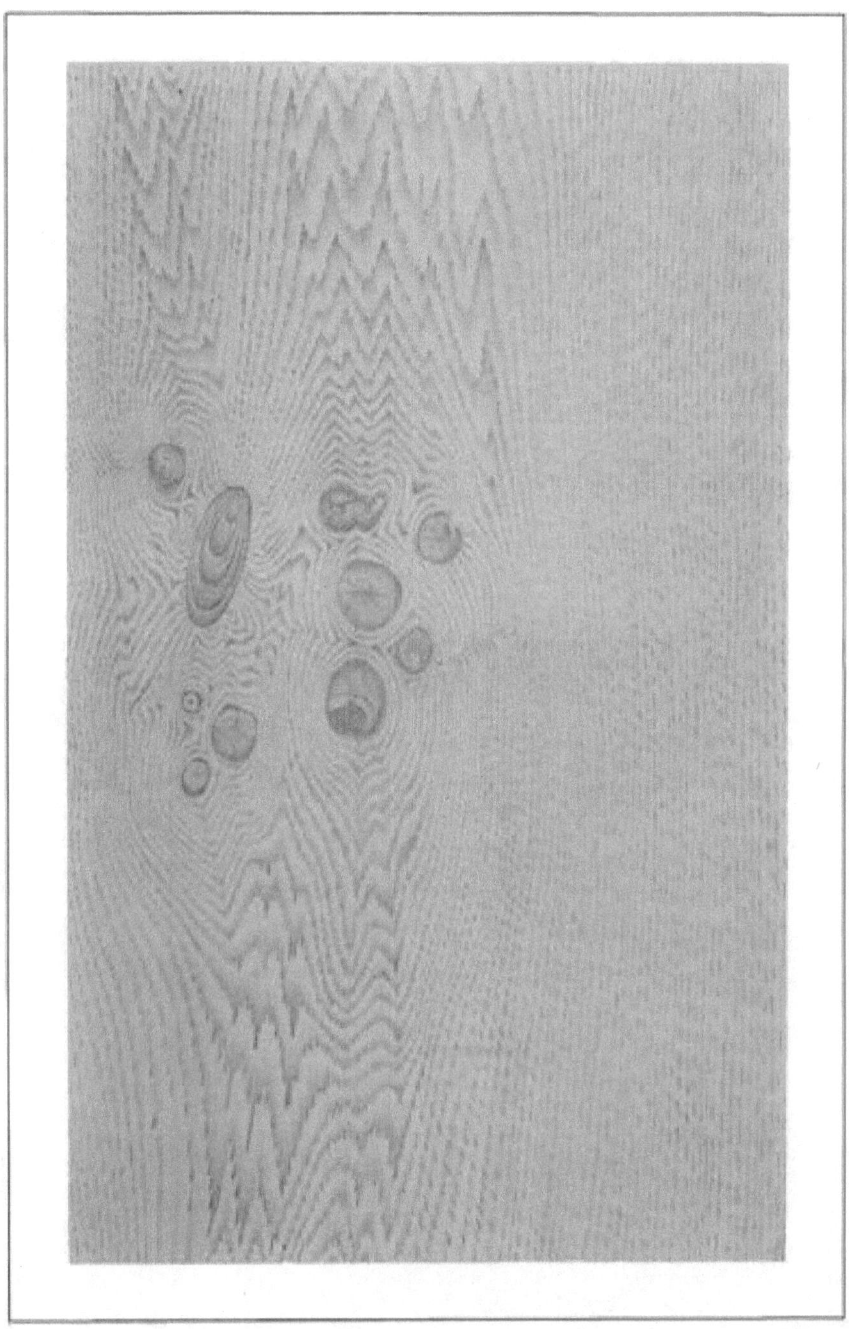

PL. 16

OAK GROWTH, SHOWING KNOTS.

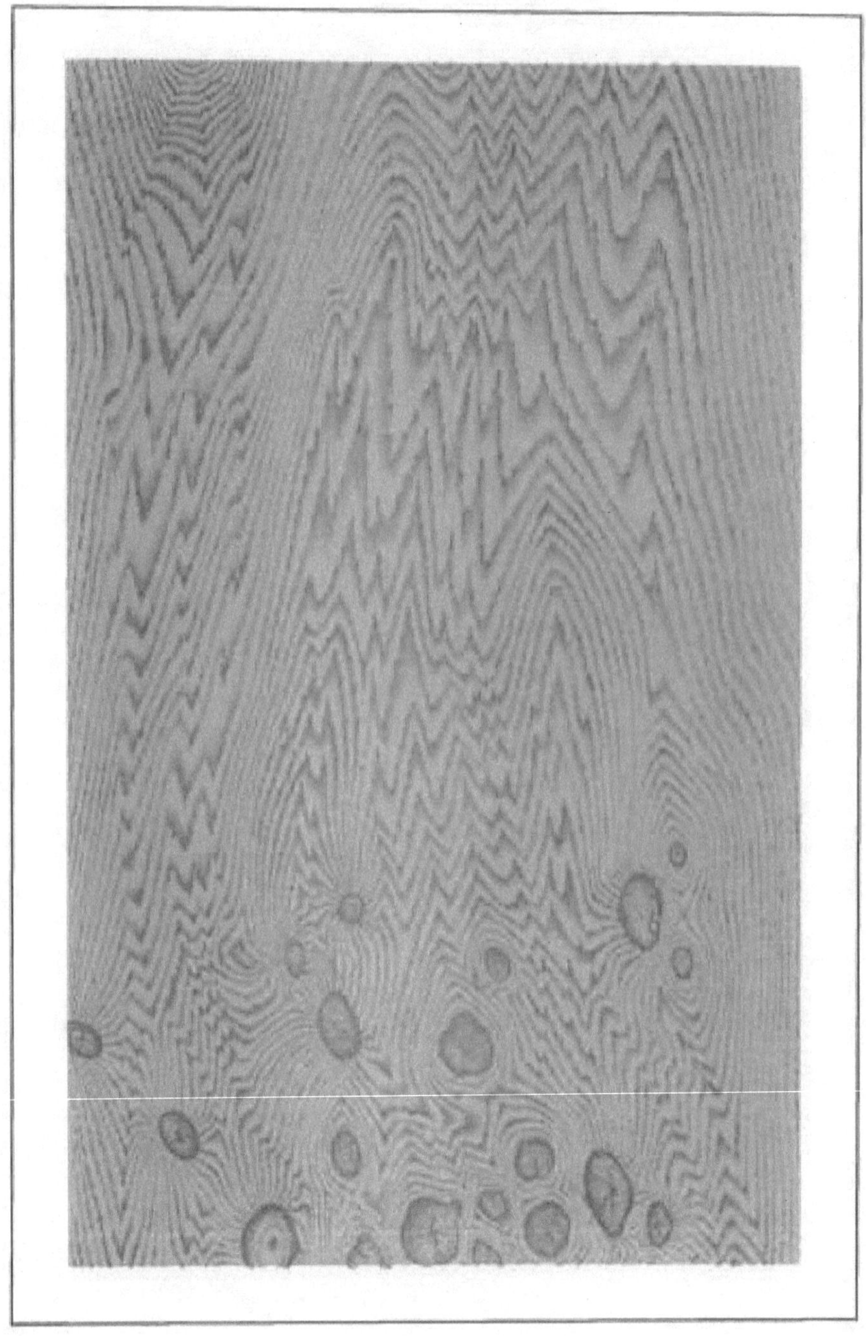

PL. 17

OAK GROWTH.

PL. 18

BLACK WALNUT GROWTH.

PL. 19

BLACK WALNUT GROWTH.

PL. 20

BLACK WALNUT GROWTH.

PL. 21

BLACK WALNUT GROWTH.

PL. 22

BLACK WALNUT GROWTH.

PL. 23

BLACK WALNUT GROWTH.

PL. 24

BLACK WALNUT GROWTH.

PL. 25

BLACK WALNUT GROWTH.

PL. 26

BLACK WALNUT GROWTH AND CROTCH.

PL. 27

FRENCH WALNUT.

PL. 28

FRENCH WALNUT.

PL. 29

ROSEWOOD.

PL. 30.

ROSEWOOD.

PL. 31
ROSEWOOD.

PL. 32

CURLED MAPLE.

PL. 33

BIRDS EYE-MAPLE.

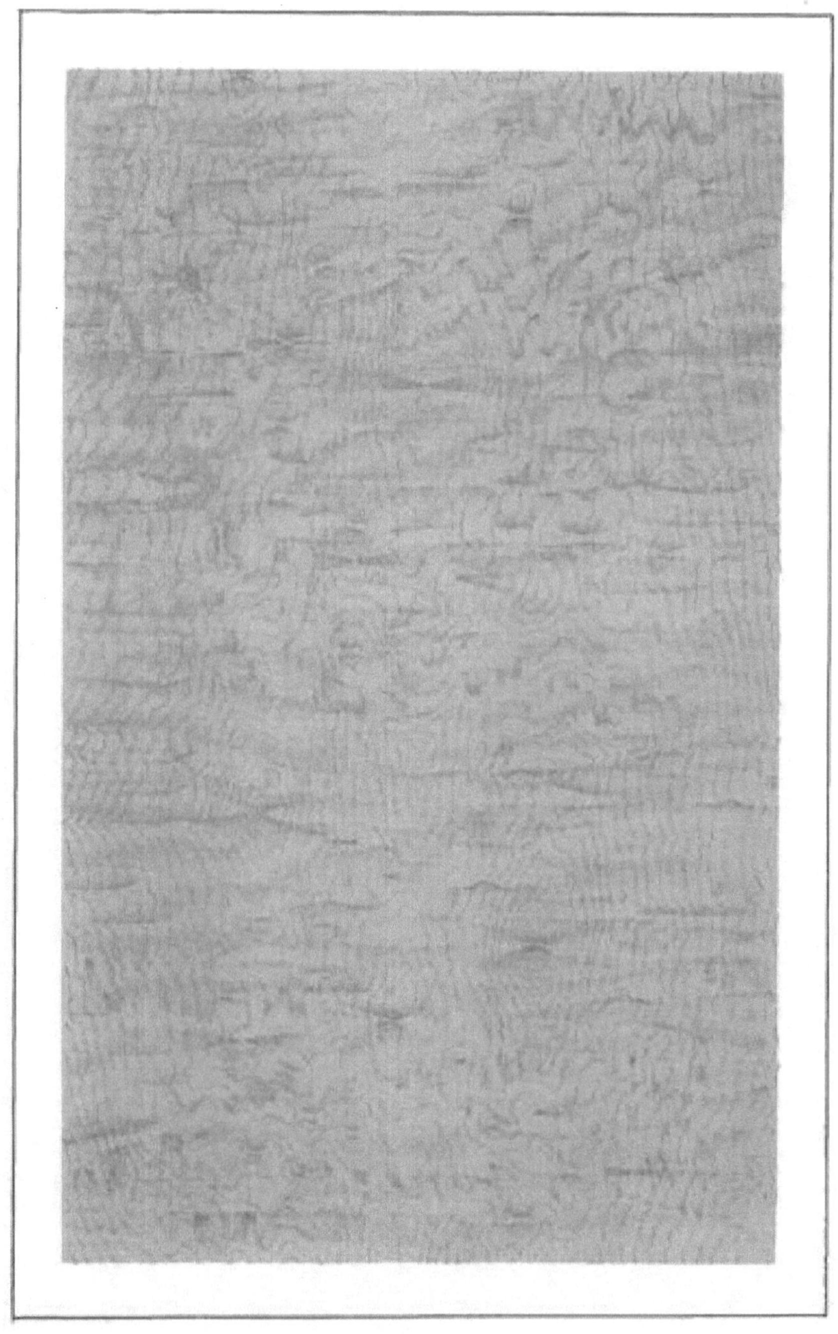

PL. 34

CURLED MAPLE.

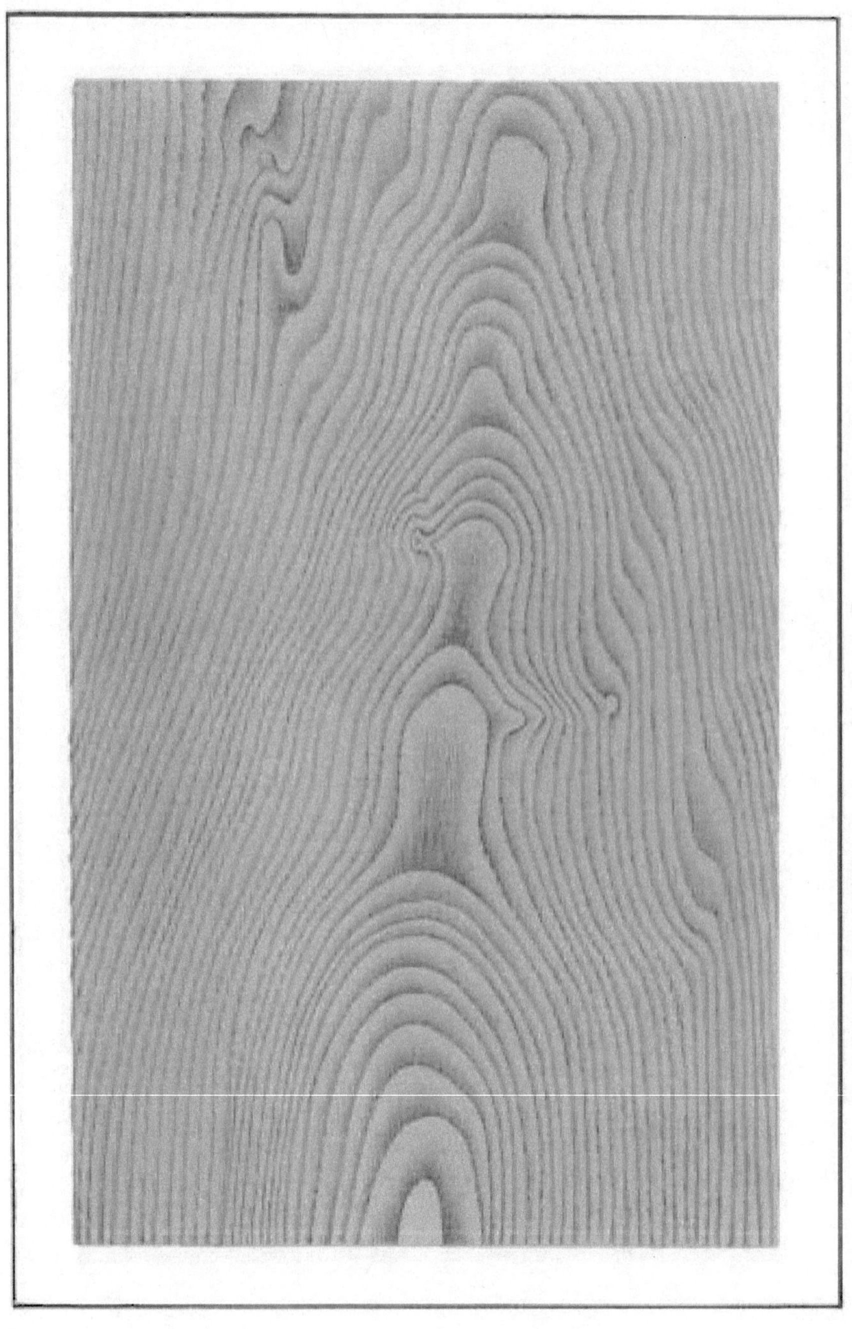

PL. 35

ASH GROWTH.

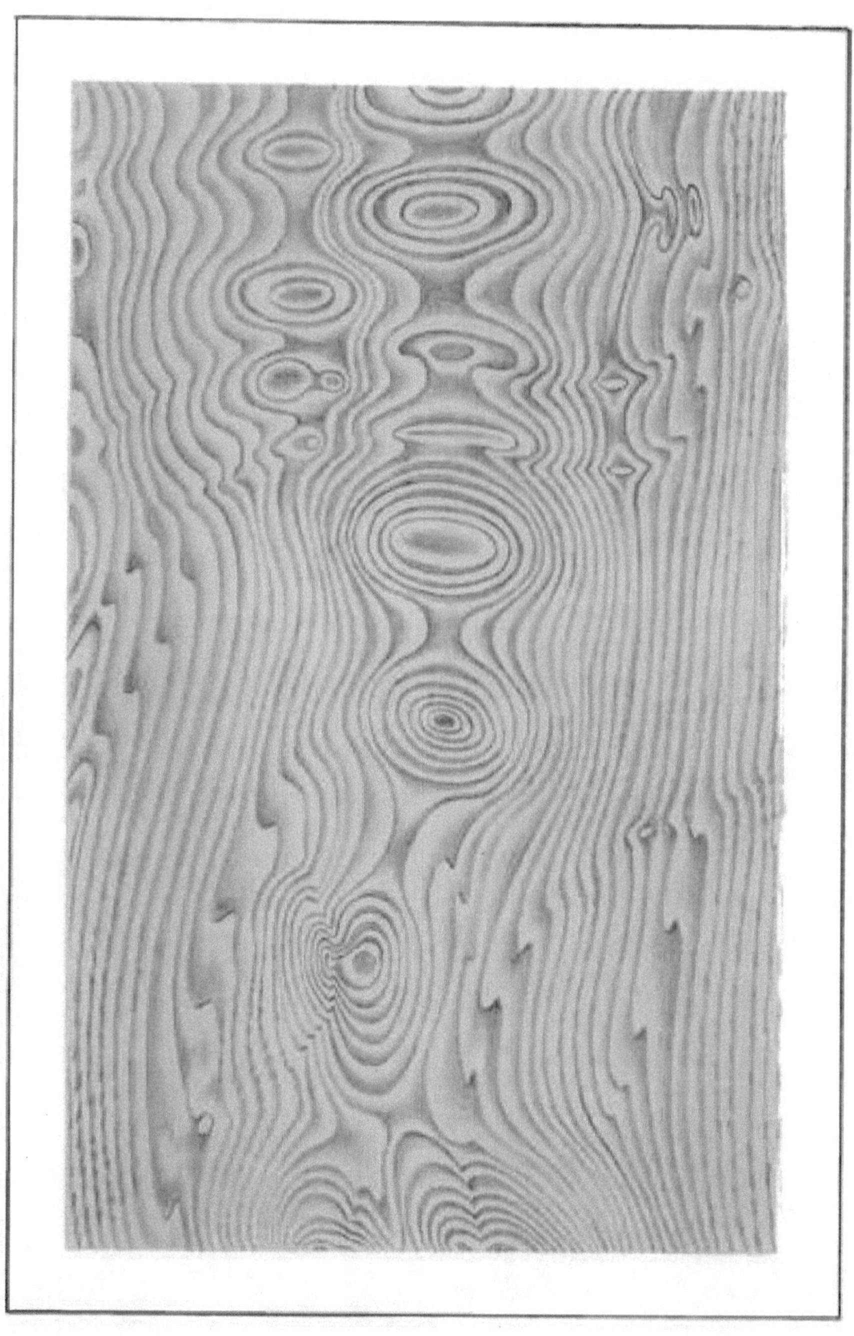

PL. 36

ASH GROWTH.

PL. 37

ASH GROWTH.

PL. 38

ASH GROWTH.

PL. 39

CHESTNUT GROWTH.

PL. 40

CHESTNUT GROWTH.

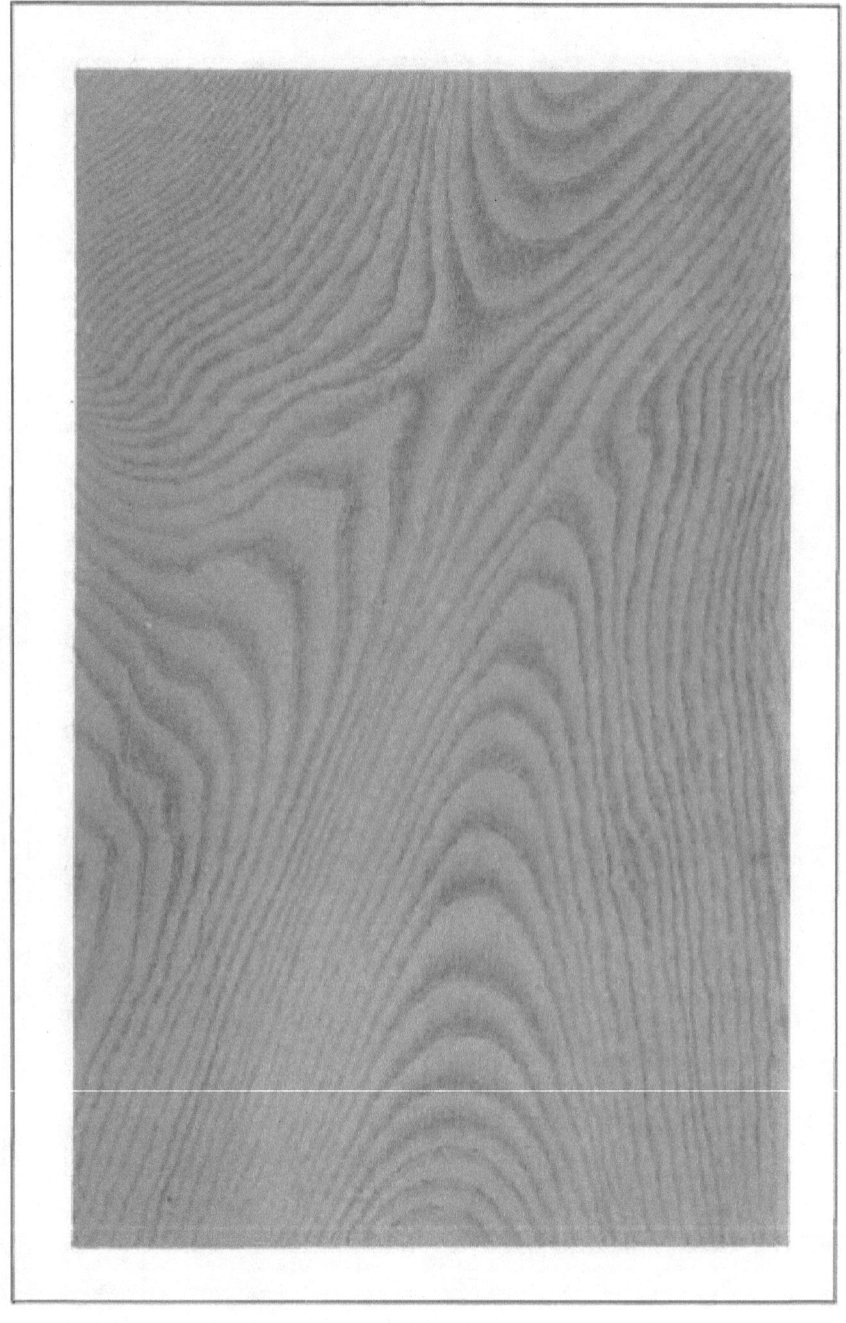

PL. 41

CHESTNUT GROWTH.

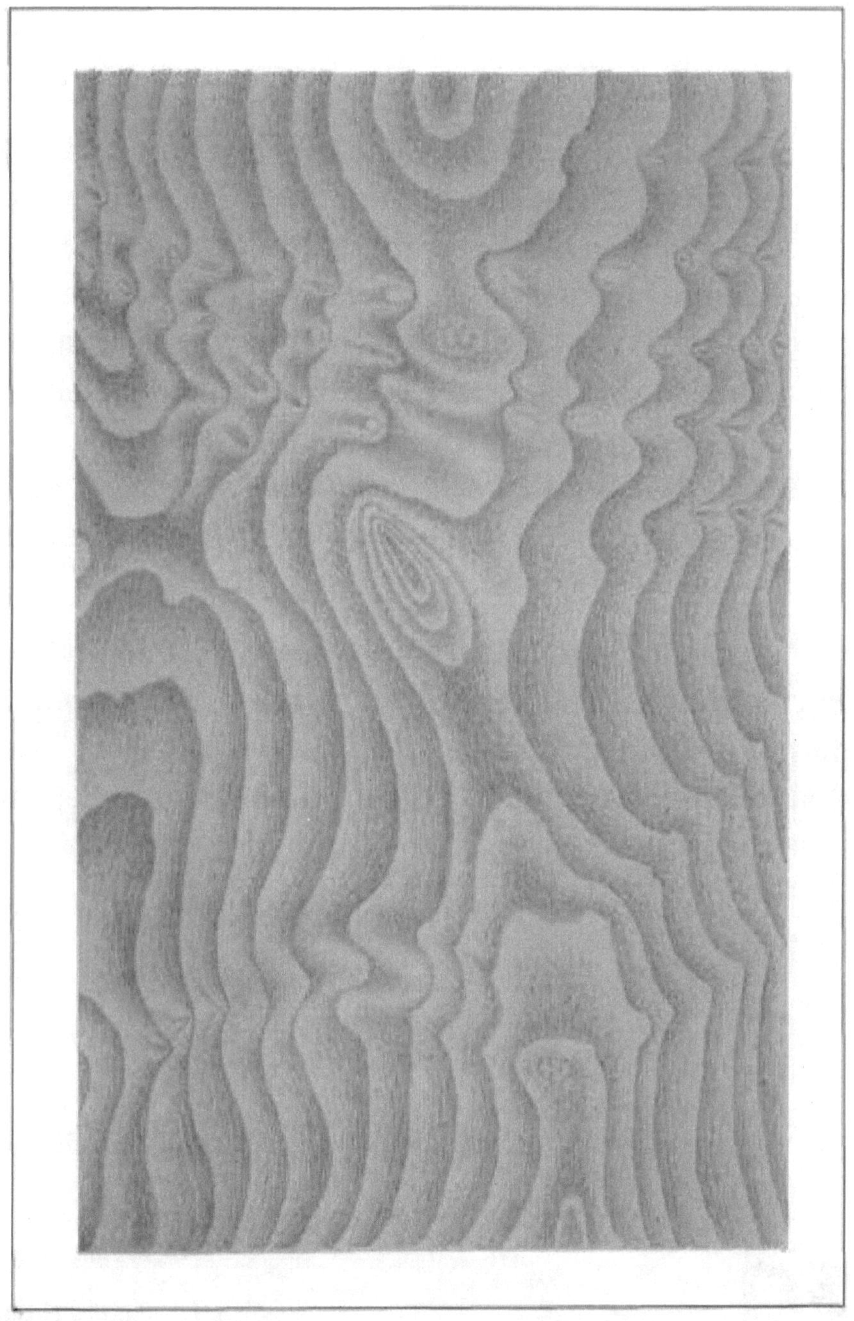

PL. 42

CHESTNUT GROWTH.

Lector House believes that a society develops through a two-fold approach of continuous learning and adaptation, which is derived from the study of classic literary works spread across the historic timeline of literature records. Therefore, we aim at reviving, repairing and redeveloping all those inaccessible or damaged but historically as well as culturally important literature across subjects so that the future generations may have an opportunity to study and learn from past works to embark upon a journey of creating a better future.

This book is a result of an effort made by Lector House towards making a contribution to the preservation and repair of original ancient works which might hold historical significance to the approach of continuous learning across subjects.

HAPPY READING & LEARNING!

LECTOR HOUSE LLP
E-MAIL: lectorpublishing@gmail.com